First World War
and Army of Occupation
War Diary
France, Belgium and Germany

40 DIVISION
121 Infantry Brigade,
Brigade Trench Mortar Battery
15 June 1916 - 31 August 1916

WO95/2616/4

The Naval & Military Press Ltd
www.nmarchive.com
Published in association with The National Archives

Published by

The Naval & Military Press Ltd

Unit 10 Ridgewood Industrial Park,

Uckfield, East Sussex,

TN22 5QE England

Tel: +44 (0) 1825 749494

www.naval-military-press.com

www.nmarchive.com

This diary has been reprinted in facsimile from the original. Any imperfections are inevitably reproduced and the quality may fall short of modern type and cartographic standards.

© Crown Copyright
Images reproduced by permission of The National Archives, London, England, 2015.

Contents

Document type	Place/Title	Date From	Date To
Heading	WO95/2616/4		
Heading	40th Division 121st Infy Bde Trench Mortar Battery Jun-Aug 1916		
War Diary	Lillers	15/06/1916	19/06/1916
War Diary	Observation.	20/06/1916	30/06/1916
War Diary	Observation.	21/06/1916	21/06/1916
Heading	War Diary Of 121st Trench Mortar Battery From 1-7-16 To 31-7-16 Volume II 40 Original July		
War Diary	Barlin	01/07/1916	03/07/1916
War Diary	Les Brebis	04/07/1916	31/07/1916
Heading	War Diary Of 121st Trench Mortar Battery From 1-8-16 To 31-8-16 Volume III		
War Diary	In The Field	01/08/1916	31/08/1916

W095/26192/4

40TH DIVISION
121ST INFY BDE

TRENCH MORTAR BATTERY

JUN - AUG 1916

40TH DIVISION
121ST INFY BDE

Confidential

Original
29/7/?

Army Form C. 2118.

WAR DIARY
of 12/3rd Trench Mortar Battery

INTELLIGENCE SUMMARY.
(Erase heading not required.)

From June 15th to June 30th

Volume I

Place	Date	Hour	Summary of Events and Information	Remarks and references to Appendices
Lillers	15.6.16	9h.	The Unit was formed and put into billets in Lillers. All ranks were drawn from Units of the Brigade.	
			Officers.	
			Lieut. F. Killinghack } 21st Middx. Regt. & Command.	
			Lieut. A.E. Markwell } 20th Middx. Regt.	
			Lieut. A.O.S. Jones. 13th Regt.	
			2/Lieut. J.W. Barrett. 12th Suffolk Regt.	
			Other Ranks. 12th Suffolk Regt. 2 Cpls. 1 Sergeant, 8 Privates	
			13th York Regt. 2 Cpls. 8 Privates	
			20th Middx Regt. 2 Cpls. 8 Privates	
			21 " " 1 Sergeant 2 Cpls. 8 Privates	
			4 Officers Servants	
"	19.6.16	7/45	Left Lillers and marched into Bailin, with the No. 8 of the Brigade and went into a hut or Observatoire, Bailin map. ref. sheet 36B. Q.15.c.	
Observatoire	20/6/16	13h.	Eight 3" Stoke Trench Mortars and six hand carts were received by us. The guns were quite new and in excellent condition. The	

Original

Confidential

WAR DIARY
of 12" Trench Mortar Battery
INTELLIGENCE SUMMARY. From June 15th June 30 2'16 Volume T (page 1?)
(Erase heading not required.)

Army Form C. 2118.

Place	Date	Hour	Summary of Events and Information	Remarks and references to Appendices
Observatoire	23/6/16	13h.	Handcarts are very heavy and will require a lot of pulling. Undoubtedly horse transport is required and will at some future date be given to the Light Trench Mortars.	
"	24/6/16	14h.	1 Officer and 10 other ranks proceeded to Les Brebis for instruction with the 1st Trench Mortar Battery in the trenches and returned 27-6-16	
"	25/6/16	16h.	3" Stokes shells were delivered to us for practice	
"	27/6/16	14h.	1 Officer and 10 other ranks proceeded to Les Brebis for instruction with the 1st French Mortar Battery and returned on 30-6-16	
"	30/6/16	"	1 Officer, 10 other ranks proceeded to Les Brebis for instruction with 1st French Mortar Battery.	
"	29/6/16	16	Lieut Killingback proceeded to Ferfay the 1st Divisional Bomb School for a course on French Mortars and returned on 29 June.	

A C Killingback
Lieut

CONFIDENTIAL.

40 ORIGINAL July Vol II

War Diary
of
121st Trench Mortar Battery

From 1-7-16 To 31-7-16

Volume II

CONFIDENTIAL

Army Form C. 2118.

Instructions regarding War Diaries and Intelligence Summaries are contained in F.S. Regs., Part II. and the Staff Manual respectively. Title pages will be prepared in manuscript.

WAR DIARY
of 121st Trench Mortar Battery
INTELLIGENCE SUMMARY.
(Erase heading not required.) from 1st-7-16 to 31-7-16

Volume II

Place	Date	Hour	Summary of Events and Information	Remarks and references to Appendices
BARLIN	1-7-16	20	Fired dummy shells and dug small emplacements	
"	2-7-16	9.	Two Officers 2/Lt Hillingback and 2/Lt Barrett went to Les Brebis to view the trenches of the 2nd Brigade with a view to taking over.	
"	3-7-16	6	121st Brigade took over from the 2nd Brigade, owing to lack of transport the battery did not arrive until 20 hrs. No 1 Section went in the line to No 2 Section remained in Les Brebis in billets taken over from 2nd Brigade	
LES BREBIS	4-7-16	20	Very quiet day. Improved emplacements, and naked shells left by 2nd Bde cleaned them and made ready for use	
"	5-7-16	20.	Worked on emplacements and cleaned our dug-out	
"	6-7-16	20.	Visited several OP's with Capt Morris Brigade Scout Officer to find suitable place for observing fire. Owing to fact that telephones are not issued to the T.M. Battery registration is very difficult	
"	7-7-16	20	All guns registered. Reported Lieut Jones to Brigadier for not taking enough interest in his work. After interviewing the Brigadier with Lieut Jones, Lieut Jones returned to his Battalion	

CONFIDENTIAL

Army Form C. 2118.

Instructions regarding War Diaries and Intelligence Summaries are contained in F.S. Regs., Part II. and the Staff Manual respectively. Title pages will be prepared in manuscript.

WAR DIARY
of 121st Trench Mortar Battery
INTELLIGENCE SUMMARY.
(Erase heading not required.)

from 1-7-16 to 31-7-16.

Volume II

Place	Date	Hour	Summary of Events and Information	Remarks and references to Appendices
LES BREBIS	8.7.16	20.	Tried to destroy enemy O.P. but owing to lack of telephone wires very difficult to get on. 2/Lieut Dowston joined for duty & to fire & place for an O.P. enemy O.P. enemy retaliated for 2 hours on Queen St and Carfax Rd.	
	9.7.16	10		
	10.7.16	13	Registered on Shrosier and made alternative emplacements	
	11.7.16	10	Enemy shelled Queen St with 77's from 13 to 13.30	
	"	13	2 Officers and 4 NCOs came to take over from 120th Brigade	
	12.7.16	17	Relieved by 120th Brigade	
	13.7.16	20	Men cleaned themselves and held kit inspection	
	14.7.16	20	to 16th-7-16, Squad drill and practice firing with dummy shells.	
	17.7.16	18	Relieved the 120th Brigade	
	18.7.16	22	Enemy retaliated to our rapid fire on THE TRIANGLE with 77's and 5.9's	
	19.7.16	13	Enemy shelled our positions we retaliated with rapid fire on all sides of THE TRIANGLE	
	21.7.16	15	We fired 5 a machine gun firing on one 8 our aeroplanes and silenced it	

CONFIDENTIAL

Army Form C. 2118.

WAR DIARY
of
INTELLIGENCE SUMMARY.
(Erase heading not required.)

121st Trench Mortar Battery
From 1st-7-16 to 31-7-16
VOLUME II

Instructions regarding War Diaries and Intelligence Summaries are contained in F. S. Regs., Part II. and the Staff Manual respectively. Title pages will be prepared in manuscript.

Place	Date	Hour	Summary of Events and Information	Remarks and references to Appendices
LES BREBIS	21.7.16	17	Made new emplacement in Boyau 7	
	22.7.16	10	Enemy sent over several T.M. bombs and rifle grenades we retaliated with 30 shells to which the enemy did not reply.	
		18	120th Brigade T.M. Batty relieved us on Right Sector Maroc.	
	23.7.16	22	Took over Loos Sector from the 48th Brigade T.M. Batty, relief completed at 20 hrs. Enemy sent over many T.M. bombs and rifle grenades.	
	24.7.16	20	All eight guns are now in the line. We retaliated with effect to Enemy T.M's and rifle grenades.	
	25.7.16	20	Very quiet day. We retaliated to a few aerial torpedoes the enemy sent over.	
	26.7.16	10	Enemy shelled King Street, we retaliated, on Triangle – quiet day.	
	27.7.16	9	Slight shelling and few rifle grenades and aerial torpedoes to which we retaliated.	
	28.7.16	8.30	Pte Dean 12468, 12th Suffolk Rgt. slightly wounded, replied effectively to aerial torpedoes	
	29.7.16	20.	Usual shelling of King St., Cordials Ave, and Queen St., we retaliated, In No 4 Sub station we heavily bombed S Cameroon Crater, Enemy ceased to work there.	
	31.7.16	21	Very quiet, slight Trench Mortar activity on No 3 Sub Section to which we retaliated.	

H.C. Killingback Lieut.
No 121 T.M.B.

ORIGINAL Vol 3

CONFIDENTIAL

War Diary
of
121st Trench Mortar Battery

From 1-8-16 To 31-8-16

Volume III

Original

Army Form C. 2118.

WAR DIARY of 121st Trench Mortar Battery
~~INTELLIGENCE~~ SUMMARY.
(Erase heading not required.) From 1-8-16 To 31-8-16

VOLUME III

Place	Date	Hour	Summary of Events and Information	Remarks and references to Appendices
In the field	1-8-16		Very quiet.	
	2."	9am	Enemy shelled King St and Queen St	
		6pm	We bombed S side of TRIANGLE but received no retaliation	
	3."	4:30am	Fired into TRIANGLE on suspected mine shaft with good effect	
		10pm	Enemy shelled Queen St and Jermyn St. We retaliated on all sides of Triangle	
	4...	7am	Enemy retaliated to our fire with heavy TM rifle grenades and aerial Torpedoes	
		9pm	Relieved by 120 Brigade Trench Mortar Battery	
	5...	10pm	Carried on with usual training during rest. Firing dummy shells.	
			Squad drill & rifle exercises until 10-8-16.	
	6.	9pm	Class started to provide qualified men to replace casualties. 1 NCO and 4 men from each battalion in the Brigade	
	10	6pm	Visited trenches to find suitable emplacements for bombing enemy trenches in co-operation with medium TM's and artillery	
	11	5pm	Relieved 120 TM Battery	
	12	4pm	Very quiet along whole of Brigade front.	
	14	5am	Damaged 3 loop holes at M/5/c 4th - 6½ Enemy retaliated on	

ORIGINAL
Army Form C. 2118.

WAR DIARY
of 121st Trench Mortar Battery
INTELLIGENCE SUMMARY
(Erase heading not required.)

From 1-8-16 To 31-8-16

VOLUME VIII

Place	Date	Hour	Summary of Events and Information	Remarks and references to Appendices
In the field	14-8-16	5 am	QUEEN ST., KING ST., and CORDIALE AVE. Enemy bombed Boyau 7 with rifle grenades and aerial torpedoes. We	
		4/o m	retaliated with our mortars and silenced them	
	15-8-16	9 am	R.W. Bennett left to attend course of medium T.M.	
	16-8-16	10.30 pm	Mortars active in Boyau 7. Cordiale Ave Enemy replied with rifle grenades and aerial torpedoes. Mortar in CORDIALE AVE was chewed but not damaged	
	17 —	11-30 am	Mortars bombed M5e 2-5½ and M10c 1-5. Enemy replied with aerial torpedoes and whizz-bangs	
	18 —	10 pm	Mortar in QUEEN ST was buried but not damaged. We bombed all sides of TRIANGLE. Enemy replied on KING ST.	
	19	2 pm	Gas test alarm was successful. Suggestion made to Brigade that the pipe of the box respirator be made longer, the for looking on the man back instead of in front so as to prevent, each mortar fired 20 rounds opening the Test alarm.	

ORIGINAL
Army Form C. 2118.

VOLUME III

WAR DIARY
of 121 Trench Mortar Batty.

INTELLIGENCE SUMMARY.
(Erase heading not required.)

From 1-8-16 To 31-8-16.

Instructions regarding War Diaries and Intelligence Summaries are contained in F.S. Regs., Part I. and the Staff Manual respectively. Title pages will be prepared in manuscript.

Place	Date	Hour	Summary of Events and Information	Remarks and references to Appendices
In the field	20.8.16	3pm	Cpl Jones 27570 of the 12th Suffolks was killed by an aerial torpedo	
	21-	4pm	Enemy bombed Queen St with aerial torpedoes and rifle grenades. We retaliated on TRIANGLE. No 21352 Cpl Brown. 12th Suffolk Regt. killed in CORDIALE AVE by heavy T.M. (Rum jar) which blew in the entrance of our dug-out, and smashed in bomb recess and emplacement.	
	22-	9am	Mortar in BOYAU 7. bombed O.P. and snipers post at M10 e 10/50. Snipers post M9 d 9½/3½ and O.P. and M.G. emplacement at M10 e 1/4½. Enemy replied only with aerial torpedoes and rifle grenades. T.M. emplacement & M5c 3/4½ Sniper post M5c/5/6. suspected T.M. emplacement. M5c 2/7. Minen shaft. Enemy replied with heavy T.M.s (Rum jar) on QUEEN St and KING St.	
	23-	4.30am	Destroyed enemy sniper post at M10 e 1-4½ with mortar in BOYAU 7. only a slight enemy retaliation	
	24	4pm	During the night we fired on M10 e 10/5 M9 D 9½/3½. Enemy retaliated with rifle grenades	
	25	4pm	Enemy bombed KING St and QUEEN St with heavy T.M.s — we retaliated	

Army Form C. 2118.

WAR DIARY
of 121st Trench Mortar Battery

INTELLIGENCE SUMMARY.
(Erase heading not required.)

From 1-8-16 To 31-8-16.

VOLUME III

Place	Date	Hour	Summary of Events and Information	Remarks and references to Appendices
In the field	25th Aug	4pm	On front line at MSC 4/3 & 4 and MOE 1-4 6t. and mine shaft at MSC 2/5.	
	26"	4pm	During the night we bombed MG emplacement MSC 5-7 and Sniper post at MSP 2/4. Several hits were observed but could not ascertain extent of damage.	
		6pm	Mortar in Boyau 7 was rendered useless by a direct hit from an aerial torpedo	
	27-	9pm	We bombed heavily on all sides of TRIANGLE and MOE 1-4½ causing much damage to enemy's wire and front line trenches	
	28-	4pm	Very quiet day. Retaliated to enemy rifle grenade and aerial torpedo	
	29	3pm	Bombed MOE 1/5 and M9a 9½/3½ with good results, smashing an enemy parapet and destroying an OP	
	30.	4pm	Bombed MOE 15, M9a 9½/3½ and MSC 6/15 with good results. Enemy did not retaliate to our fire	
	31-	4pm	Mortars in King St. & Queen St. fired on TRIANGLE. Enemy retaliated with rifle grenades only.	

K.O. Killingback Capt.
O/C 121st T.M.B.

www.ingramcontent.com/pod-product-compliance
Lightning Source LLC
Chambersburg PA
CBHW081617160426
43191CB00011B/2163